THE
MIDDLE AGES

THE MIDDLE AGES

PETER
BEDRICK
BOOKS

This edition published in 2002 by Peter Bedrick Books
an imprint of McGraw-Hill Children's Publishing
8787 Orion Place
Columbus, OH 43240

ISBN 1-57768-952-6

Printed in China

McGraw-Hill
Children's Publishing

A Division of The McGraw·Hill Companies

PHOTOGRAPHIC CREDITS

11 (T/R) British Museum, London/ The Bridgeman Art Library; 21 (B/R) Robert Harding Picture
Library; 29 (T/R) Wolfgang Kaehler/CORBIS; (T/L) Bettmann/CORBIS; 31 (T/R) Bettmann/CORBIS,
(T/L) Archivo Iconografico, S.A./CORBIS; 43 (B/L) Historical Picture Archive/ CORBIS; 44, (C) Archivo
Iconografico, S.A./ CORBIS; 46 (B/L) Archivo Iconografico, S.A./CORBIS. All other images from the Miles
Kelly Archive.

QUOTATION ACKNOWLEDGMENTS

Page 17 (translated by Frank O'Connor), published in *World Poetry* by W. W. Norton and Company; pages 9,
31, 33, 47 published in the *Oxford Dictionary of Quotations* by the Oxford University Press; page 11, extract from
Ecclesiastical History of the English Nation, published in Internet Medieval Sourcebook, Fordham University Centre
for Medieval Studies; page 14, extract from *Whole Works*, published by Jubilee Edition; page 45 quoted in
Millennium, edited by Anthony Coleman, published by Bantam Press.

Every effort has been made to trace all copyright holders and obtain permissions. The
editor and publishers sincerely apologize for any inadvertent errors or omissions and will be happy to correct
them in any future editions.

Contents

The advance of Islam seemed unstoppable in the late 600s. The Byzantine and Persian empires could not halt the armies of Islam, nor could Egypt. By AD 700, Muslims controlled most of the North African coast, and ships patrolled the Mediterranean Sea and Indian Ocean.

Muslim Empires

Muslims from Morocco invaded Spain, but the advance of Islam into western Europe was stopped in AD 732 by the Frankish army of Charles Martel.

Life under Ummayad rule

Under the rule of the Ummayad family in Damascus there were four classes of citizens: Arabian Muslims; new converts; Christians, Jews, and Mandaeans (a Persian sect); and slaves. The new converts included people from Egypt, Syria, Persia, and Asia Minor. They adopted Arab ways but brought to the Arabs a wealth of new learning in philosophy, medicine, art, and science.

Islam had been born in the desert. The Ummayad court was a more sophisticated world where music and gambling were tolerated. One caliph married a Christian. Another spent most of his time horse racing.

The Abbasid Empire

Ummayad rule grew weaker but lasted until the mid-700s. Then Abu al Abbas, a descendant of Muhammad, founded a new dynasty – the Abbasids. His followers raised an army in Persia and rallied the supporters of the dead caliph Ali to their cause. After a terrible battle lasting nine

▷ A scene from The Thousand and One Nights, a collection of stories set in the Baghdad court of Harun al-Rashid, the most famous of the Abbasid rulers. In these stories, collected from around the eastern world, characters such as Sinbad and Aladdin appear.

AD 632	Abu Bakr becomes first caliph.
AD 644	Caliph Omar is murdered and is succeeded by Otham, leader of the Ummayad.
AD 656	Othman is murdered and the Shiite leader Ali becomes caliph.
AD 661	Ali is murdered. The Islamic capital moves from Mecca to Damascus.
AD 685–705	Caliph Abdalmalik sets up new government system for the Islamic empire.
AD 732	Franks defeat Muslims at battle of Poitiers to halt their advance into Europe.
AD 750	The Abbasid dynasty is founded.
AD 786	Harun al-Rashid unites the Islamic empire.
AD 1000s	Turkish Seljuks seize power in Baghdad.

▷ *Arab trading ships sailed across the Indian Ocean to India and Indonesia and farther eastward as far as China.*

△ *An Arab astronomer's drawing of the star group, or constellation, of Orion (the Hunter). Like the Greeks, Arab scientists drew constellations as human figures, animals, or objects.*

days, they captured Damascus. Most of the Ummayad ruling family was murdered, and the new rulers soon moved their capital to Baghdad (in what is now Iraq).

Arabic was the common language throughout most of the Islamic world. By AD 786, the court of the caliph Harun al-Rashid at Baghdad was one of the most splendid in the world. Trading ships sailed to and from China, and the warehouses along the River Tigris were stocked with rare and wonderful goods from Africa, India, and the Far East. Medicine and science were ahead of anything known in Europe. There were slaves from Africa and even Scandinavia.

Rival rulers, however, claimed independence in various parts of this empire. Baghdad itself came under threat in the 11th century from invaders.

The Seljuk Empire

The Seljuks were descendants of nomadic Turks from central Asia. They took their name from a chief named Seljuk. They charged into the western Islamic world in the early AD 1000s. Their leader Toghril Beg captured Baghdad. His nephew Alp Arslan attacked the city of Constantinople and defeated the Byzantine army in AD 1071.

The Seljuks

The Turkish Seljuks were superb horsemen, riding with stirrups and firing bows at the gallop. Known as "the men of the sword," they added new strength to Islam, which was governed by "the men of the law."

△ *The crescent moon and star became important symbols in Islam and were often incorporated into architecture and other designs. The Islamic year calendar is based on the cycle of the Moon.*

After the fall of the Roman Empire, the Christian church provided the only stable government in Europe. It was weakened by its division, between the west (Rome) and the east (Constantinople) and faced growing pressure from the spread of Islam.

Monastic Life

The Christian faith spread slowly among the pagan peoples of western and northern Europe, who were called "heathens" by Christians. Its teachings were spread by missionaries, such as Patrick, Augustine, and Boniface. Missionaries traveled to the British Isles, Germany, Scandinavia, and Russia, converting the local rulers and building churches. It was a slow business, and parts of northern Europe were not Christian until the beginning of the second millennium.

Egyptian missionaries preach in Ethiopia.	AD 350
St. Patrick preaches Christianity in Ireland.	AD 450
St. Columba founds a monastery on the island of Iona.	AD 500s
St. Benedict of Nursia sets the rules for Western monks.	AD 480–543
Monte Cassino in Italy is the first abbey in Europe.	AD 529
Pope Gregory sends Augustine to convert the English.	AD 596
Augustine founds the first English Benedictine monastery at Canterbury.	AD 596
Boniface preaches to the Saxons in Germany.	C. AD 700
Edward the Confessor starts to build Westminster Abbey.	AD 1042

Christian communities took on the work of teaching faith, education, and healing, at a time when governments themselves had very little power. In this work, monasteries came to play an important part.

Saint Benedict's rules

In the early Christian world, very religious people had sometimes gone off to live on their own as hermits, to

▷ A monk at work on an illuminated manuscript (handwritten book). The work was slow and painstaking but worthwhile because it was another way to show dedication to God.

△ The monastery at Mont Saint-Michel in France was built by Benedictine monks in AD 966. It stands on a tiny island in Normandy, linked by causeway to the French mainland.

△ Monks spent part of their time teaching young boys, who would in time become monks themselves. A monk's day was regulated by hours of work, rest, and worship.

△ An "illuminated" letter from the page of a medieval manuscript. Monastery artists and scribes decorated the pages of their books with these beautifully colored "illuminations."

Celtic Christians

Elaborate carvings were made on Celtic crosses, the distinctive symbol of the Celtic Christians. They founded monasteries in the north of Britain. One of the first, at Lindisfarne, was founded in AD 635 by a monk named Aidan.

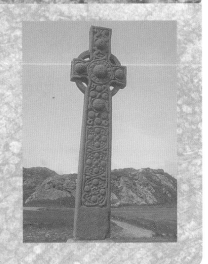

meditate and pray. Others formed strict communities, where they lived apart, praying and studying the Bible, hoping to avoid the "sins" of town life. These communities became monasteries.

In the AD 500s, an Italian named Benedict of Nursia drew up a set of rules for monks (people in monasteries). All monks must be poor, unmarried, and obedient. Monks wore simple robes, shaved their heads, and shared all their the daily tasks.

Monasteries were for men only. Religious women joined orders of their own and became nuns. Each monastery was led by an abbot, and the largest ones became centers not only of religious life but also of local power. Some abbots had as much power as any nobleman, controlling farms, trades, and even private armies.

The daily round

Monks went to eight church services every day. They ate their meals in the refectory, the dining room, often in silence while one monk read from the Bible or some other religious book. They grew their food, reared farm animals, baked bread, and brewed beer. They made their clothes and furniture and built their own churches. They also looked after the sick.

There is no salvation outside the Church.
Love the sinner but hate the sin.
Love and do what you will.

ST. AUGUSTINE OF HIPPO (AD 354-430)

St. Augustine was born in what is now Tunisia in Africa. He was one of the most important men in the early Christian Church.

In the late AD 300s, the Roman army was hard pressed to fight off waves of barbarian invasions. Troops in distant outposts, such as the British Isles, were needed to defend the empire, and by AD 410, the last Roman soldiers had left England for mainland Europe.

Britain After the Romans

The Romans had hired warriors from northwest Europe (Germany and Denmark) to help defend the coasts of England against pirates and raiding bands (many of whom were Germans themselves). Without the Roman army to protect them, the Roman Britons of England were unable to prevent these mercenaries, and any new bands of invaders, from taking over land they wanted.

Roman army has left Roman Britain by this date.	AD 410
Possible date of "King Arthur," leader of the Britons.	AD 500
Augustine arrives to convert the English to Christianity.	AD 597
Death of Redwald, king of East Anglia. Sutton Hoo ship burial.	c. AD 627
Lifetime of English monk Bede, who wrote a history of the English people.	AD 673–735
Offa of Mercia is overlord of all England.	AD 780
First Viking attacks on England.	AD 787
Kenneth MacAlpin is first king of a united Scotland.	AD 843
Rhodri Mawr is Prince of Wales.	AD 844

The newcomers were a mixture of peoples – Angles, Saxons, Jutes, Frisians – who became known as the "English." There were also raiders from the north, Picts and Scots, who attacked northern England.

The Saxon settlement

The invaders came to England to find land to farm. They were well armed and tough and drove away many Britons, who moved into western England and Wales, taking their Christianity with them. The pagan newcomers took over their farms but also set about clearing new land. They felled trees, plowed the land, and built wooden houses.

The new English were suspicious of Roman-British civilization and avoided the towns. Gradually these towns fell into decay. Roads were no longer used, and Roman villas, their owners gone, became ruins – empty reminders of a vanished way of life.

△ *A Scots warrior. The Scots' leader, Kenneth MacAlpin, was the first king to rule the land we now call Scotland.*

Sutton Hoo

Artifacts from the Sutton Hoo burial site include a gold belt, a sword, and a shield. There are also several pieces of jewelery. Finally, there was a scepter and standard which must have belonged to the dead King Redwald.

The English kings

By AD 600, the English had set up several small kingdoms. These included Kent, East Anglia, Essex, Sussex and Wessex ("the lands of the East, South, and West Saxons"), Mercia, and Northumbria.

The most powerful ruler among the English kings was acknowledged as "bretwalda," or supreme king. The Sutton Hoo ship burial, discovered in AD 1939, is almost certainly the monument to King Redwald of East Anglia, who was bretwalda in the AD 620s, and who died in AD 627. The strongest English king of the AD 700s was Offa of Mercia.

Western and northern Britain

In Wales, there were four British kingdoms: Gywnedd, Dyfed, Powys, and Gwent. These were independent under their own princes. In the west of England was the kingdom of Dumnonia. In the far north, the Picts ruled Pictavia and fought the Scots who ruled in the west. By the AD 800s, the Scots, under Kenneth MacAlpin, claimed to rule the Picts as well.

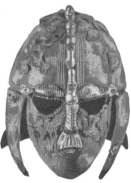

△ *The iron helmet found in the ship burial at Sutton Hoo is one of many treasures unearthed by archaeologists at the site in Suffolk.*

△ *Saxon farmers harvested grain with sickles and pitchforks. The Saxons tilled old Roman fields and plowed new land but abandoned the Roman villas.*

At this period ... Britain, being deprived ... of all her warlike stores, and of the flower of her army, was exposed to the ravages of her enemies on every side.

ECCLESIASTICAL HISTORY, ST. BEDE (AD 731)

Bede was a monk in the AD 700s. He wrote an important book called the Ecclesiastical History of the English People.

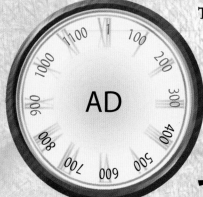

The Franks emerged from the ruins of the Roman Empire in AD 476 as the dominant people of western Europe. Their leader Clovis enlarged his lands around the River Rhine (Germany) by wars. By AD 540, the Franks ruled most of the old Roman province of Gaul (France, named after the Franks).

The Franks

The first Frankish ruling family is known as the Merovingian dynasty, after Clovis's grandfather Meroveus. Clovis became a Christian. He made Paris his capital city. Most of the Franks were peasant farmers, who lived on lands ruled by nobles. The peasants raised food, doing the seasonal tasks of plowing, sowing, and harvesting. They also had to fight for their lord when he went to war. Frankish lords fought to win new land and shared the spoils of conquest with their soldiers. This Frankish system of land-holding and service was the beginning of the feudal system in Europe.

Clovis becomes king of the Franks.	AD 481
Franks defeat the last great Roman army in the West at the battle of Soissons.	AD 486
Franks control most of Gaul and Germany.	AD 540
Pepin the Short founds the Carolingian dynasty.	AD 751
Charlemagne born.	C. AD 742
Charlemagne rules the Franks.	AD 771
Charlemagne fights Muslims in Spain. The Frankish army is attacked at Roncesvalles.	AD 778
Charlemagne is crowned emperor of the West by Pope Leo III.	AD 800
Charlemagne dies.	AD 814

The Carolingians

The Merovingian kings actually had less power than their "mayors of the royal palace," officials who traditionally came from two families. The winner of a power struggle between these families was Pepin of Herstal, who ruled the

▷ Charlemagne was very tall and a man of enormous energy. He could not write, but he did learn to read Latin. He liked to listen as books were read to him.

12

▷ Frankish soldiers head for battle. Under Charlemagne, the Frankish Empire expanded greatly, taking in neighboring Bavaria and Lombardy. The Franks finally conquered Saxony after about 30 years of bitter fighting.

△ The sword of Charlemagne. The favorite weapons of Frankish soldiers were the lance and the sword.

Franks even though he was not their king. Pepin's son was Charles Martel, whose army defeated the Muslim invaders of southern Europe in AD 632. Charles Martel's son was another Pepin, Pepin the Short, and he made himself king.

Pepin the Short's son Charles became the most famous of all Frankish rulers. He was called Carolus Magnus (Charles the Great), or Charlemagne in old French. The "Carolingian" dynasty is named after him.

Charlemagne's empire

When Pepin died, his sons Carloman and Charlemagne shared power until Carloman died. Then Charlemagne set out and won new wars of conquest in the Netherlands, Germany, and Italy. When he defeated pagans, such as the Saxons of Germany, he forced them to become Christians like himself.

Charlemagne wanted to govern well. His capital of Aachen, called "a second Rome," was rich and dazzling, yet he chose to live simply. No other ruler in Europe was so famous or magnificent, and on Christmas Day in 800, the pope crowned Charlemagne Holy Roman

New writing

This is a sample of Carolingian script, the clear and more easily written style of writing that was introduced during the reign of Charlemagne. The actual text is written in Latin.

△ The horn of Roland, a Frankish hero killed at the battle of Roncesvalles in AD 778.

The power of the English kingdoms ebbed and flowed as first one, then another, became dominant. By AD 800, the strongest English kingdom was Wessex. But it faced a threat from yet more invaders, the Vikings, who saw England as a good place to settle.

Alfred the Great

The Vikings came from Norway, Sweden, and Denmark. The first Viking ships appeared off the southern English coast in AD 787, according to the history known as the Anglo-Saxon Chronicle, which was begun in the reign of Alfred.

Northern Britain, too, felt the fury of these marauding Norsemen, or Danes as the English called them. Vikings raided and looted the rich monasteries of Northumbria. Ships loaded with families and farm animals also crossed the North Sea, and Viking farmers and traders settled in Orkney, in Ireland, and the Isle of Man.

A fight for survival

In AD 850, a huge fleet of 350 Viking ships appeared in the River Thames. That winter a Viking army camped in southeast England for the first time. Such mass attacks posed a threat to the survival of the English kingdoms.

East Anglia, Northumbria, and Mercia were all ravaged by Viking armies in the AD 860s. The Christian king of East Anglia, King Edmund, was murdered for refusing to give up his faith. In AD 871, Wessex was attacked. Its new king was the young and untested Alfred, the fifth of four brothers, each of whom had been king before him.

Alfred's wars and peace

Alfred's first campaigns were failures, and he had to retreat and hide in the

First Vikings land in England.	AD 787
Alfred is born.	AD 849
A great army of Vikings attacks England.	AD 865
Vikings kill King Edmund of East Anglia.	AD 869
Alfred becomes king of Wessex.	AD 871
Alfred captures London and fortifies the city.	AD 886
Alfred dies. His son Edward becomes king (to AD 924).	AD 899
Athelstan, Alfred's grandson, rules English and Vikings in England.	AD 924
Reign of Edgar, the high point of Anglo-Saxon rule in England.	AD 959–975

AD

△ Alfred had fought at sea himself and ordered the building of ships for the first English navy. The new ships were similar to the Viking longships, but bigger and faster.

14

△ *Alfred is said to have made candle clocks to time his working day, which was divided between government, prayer, and learning.*

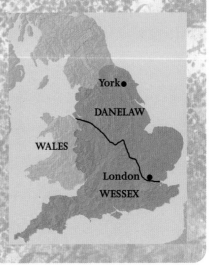

The Danelaw

The lands in eastern England settled by the Vikings became known as the Danelaw. The English at the time referred to the invaders as "Danes." In places, Viking settlers mingled with the local people.

marshes of Somerset. Rallying his forces, he defeated the Vikings at the battle of Edington and made a treaty with them. The Viking leader Guthrum agreed to become a Christian. In return, Alfred allowed the Vikings to settle in East Anglia.

Alfred was now recognized as king of all the English. He set about making his kingdom strong enough to resist future Viking attacks. He built a navy. He built forts and fortified towns called burhs to protect the countryside. He rebuilt the defences of London. He organized a system of "call-up" in time of war – a farmer had to supply two soldiers for every plow on his land. The army was divided into two groups: one armed and ready to fight, the other working on farms and guarding the forts.

Law-maker and scholar

Alfred issued new laws, to end the feuds which caused bloodshed between families and to give more protection to the weak against the strong. He divided his kingdom into shires governed by eldermen.

Alfred invited foreign scholars to his court. He was determined to educate his people, and he spent many hours translating books from Latin into English. For his many achievements, he is the only English king honored with the title "the Great."

△ *The Alfred jewel was found near Athelney in Somerset in AD 1693. It may be part of a bookmark. On it are the words "Alfred had me made" in Latin.*

> Then began I . . . to turn into English the book that is named in Latin *Pastoralis* . . . one-while word for word, another-while meaning for meaning.

ALFRED THE GREAT (AD 849–899)

Alfred was the most important lawmaker among England's early kings.

The Vikings came from Scandinavia (Norway, Denmark, and Sweden). Their homeland of mountains, fjords, and forests offered little spare farmland for a growing population. So, many Vikings went abroad in search of new lands to settle.

The Vikings

The Vikings were farmers, but also fierce warriors, and their first impact on western Europe was a violent one. Norwegians and Danes began to sail across the North Sea in the late AD 700s, raiding the coasts of Britain and mainland Europe. They raided churches and towns, carrying off loot and slaves. Their raids caused panic, and rulers tried to buy off the invaders with gold. This only encouraged the Vikings to come back for more.

Trade and home life

Viking towns such as Kaupang in Norway and Hedeby in Denmark flourished on deals in furs, reindeer antlers, and walrus ivory. These materials were exchanged for weapons, jewels, and pottery.

Viking home life was based on farming and fishing. Several generations (including uncles and cousins) often shared one single-roomed house made of wood, stone, or turf. A good sword was passed down from father to son.

Many of the Vikings' gods were the same pagan gods of the Germans and English. The most important was one-eyed Odin, but most people's favorite was Thor, the thunder god who brandished his hammer.

The trading town of Hedeby in Denmark is founded.	AD 790s
First reported Viking raid on England.	AD 787
Vikings begin to settle in the Baltic region and Russia.	AD 860
Vikings reach Iceland.	AD 874
Vikings are given Normandy to prevent further attacks on France.	AD 911
Danish Vikings become Christians.	AD 960
Erik the Red discovers Greenland.	AD 982
Leif Eriksson lands in North America.	AD 1003
A Dane, Cnut, becomes king of England.	AD 1016

△ Ships lie beached beside a Viking town, with wooden houses thatched with straw. Vikings made long journeys by ship and overland to trade.

Longships

The Viking longships were fast and strong enough to cross oceans. They had a long, slender hull with a single mast and sail.

△ Both Viking men and women dressed in hard-wearing clothing made from linen or woolen cloth. They wore shoes made from leather.

Intrepid voyagers

Sailing west into the Atlantic Ocean, Norwegian Vikings settled in Iceland (AD 874) and Greenland (AD 982), and they landed in North America in AD 1003. Swedish Vikings crossed the Baltic to the important trade towns of Kiev and Novgorod and traveled on eastward to the Black Sea. Greek and Arab merchants called the northerners "Rus" – which is how Russia got its name.

Vikings could be found in Sicily, Baghdad, and Constantinople. Trade goods from such faraway places have been found in Jorvik (York) in England and in Dublin in Ireland.

Leaders and government

The leader of each community was the richest landowner, or jarl. He shared his wealth, entertaining his warriors and servants with feasts and songs in his great hall. The most powerful leaders called themselves kings. They tried to settle blood feuds between enemies, which were very common.

Viking free men met in assemblies called "things" to settle disputes about crimes or land disagreements. Laws passed down from generation to generation. A person who refused to obey the rules of the "thing" was an outlaw, and anyone might kill him.

Since tonight the wind is high/ The sea's white mane a fury/ I need not fear the hordes of Hell/ Coursing the Irish Channel.

ON THE VIKING RAIDS, ANONYMOUS

△ Decorative brooches such as this were used by both Viking men and women to hold their outer garments (cloaks and tunics) in place.

By the AD 1000s, trade routes between Europe and Asia were well established. Much of this trade went by sea. People traded in slaves and furs, gold and silver, ivory and precious stones, silk and carpets, glass and leatherwork.

Trade and Towns

Arab dhows sailed to India and East Africa, Chinese junks to the islands of Indonesia and Japan. Viking ships crossed the Atlantic to Iceland, Greenland, and North America. The Vikings founded small settlements. In Iceland, settlers met in the Althing – Europe's oldest democratic assembly.

By land and sea

Many sea craft were small, with oars and could navigate rivers; river towns were often busy ports, like London and Viking Jorvik (York), for example. There was regular trade between Vikings in Jorvik and Dublin in Ireland, with Viking towns in Scandinavia.

Few poor people ever left their home village except perhaps to go to market. But scholars, soldiers, merchants, and kings traveled far, even though roads were poor. Charlemagne traveled widely around his empire. King Alfred went from England to Rome as a boy. Most journeys were made on foot, or on horseback, and were slow. Travelers followed well-used

△ Merchants exchange goods in a busy street in Viking Jorvik (modern York) in England. These men are trading in furs, which were one of the main exports of Jorvik at this time.

AD	
Paper-making spreads from China into the Islamic world.	AD 750
Porcelain is first made in China.	AD 900
Trade treaties are made between Kiev and Constantinople.	AD 907
An Arab scholar, Al-Masudi, travels the East African coast as far south as Mozambique.	AD 916
Rise of the kingdom of Ghana in Africa and its chief city Kumbi Saleh.	AD 920
Woodblock printing of inexpensive books in China.	AD 950
First Viking sighting of North American mainland.	AD 1000
Ghana kingdom controls trade routes across the Sahara in Africa.	AD 1000
Leif Eriksson lands in North America.	AD 1003

▷ Caravans carrying gold, salt, and slaves followed the long trails across the Sahara Desert. There was trade between the cities of West Africa and those of North Africa, Egypt, and Arabia. The routes taken by Muslim pilgrims to Mecca in Arabia were also important.

trade routes, where some safety from bandits might be expected. The most famous was the Silk Road, the long trade route overland from China to the west.

How peoples saw themselves

By AD 1000, the Christian peoples of Europe were taught to see themselves as belonging to "Christendom" – the Christian world. In its empire, Islam had unified peoples who shared not only a religion but also language, science, and art.

To an Easterner, Western civilization appeared much less sophisticated. An Arab ambassador seeing Vikings in Russia thought them impressive ("as tall as date palms"), but uncivilized – they ate like animals, lived in crude houses, and worshipped idols.

Civilizations apart

With their canals, fine houses, markets, and restaurants, Chinese cities were unrivaled. Yet, China remained aloof, caring little for what went on in the barbarian world beyond its frontiers. The peoples of North and South America, too, remained outside the growing cultural exchange.

△ Odin, the god of battle and death, was one of the principal gods worshiped by the Vikings. He was the ruler of Asgard, the heavenly home of the gods.

Silk traders

For many years, the Chinese were the only people that knew how to make silk. European traders would make the long journey to China to take silk back to Europe, where it was an expensive luxury.

△ A pottery figure of an Armenian merchant, made in China during the Tang dynasty (AD 618–907).

In the AD 900s, England was again attacked by Vikings. King Ethelred (AD 978–1016) tried to buy off the invaders with bribes. His people had to pay higher taxes to raise the money. But the idea of bribes did not work either.

Norman Conquest

In AD 1013, the Danish king Sweyn Forkbeard made himself king of England, and the unpopular Ethelred fled to Normandy in France. In AD 1016, Sweyn's son Cnut became king. During his reign, which lasted until AD 1035, England was ruled as part of Cnut's empire, which included Denmark and Norway. Cnut was a good king, but his two sons had brief reigns, and England's next ruler brought confusion.

Edward the Confessor

The new king was Edward, known as the Confessor, son of the exiled Etheltred. He was more Norman than English and very religious. He built the first Westminster Abbey.

Power was in the hands of the English earls, like the scheming Godwine of Wessex. Edward married Godwine's daughter, but they had no children. So when Edward died in AD 1066, there was no obvious heir. The witan, or council, of England chose Earl Godwine's son, Harold, as king.

Rivals for a crown

There were two other claimants. One was Harold Hardrada, king of Norway. The other was William, Duke of Normandy, a distant relative of Edward the Confessor. William claimed that Harold had sworn to

Viking leader Rollo is given Normandy. Normandy is later ruled by dukes.	AD 911
King Cnut, ruler of England, Norway, and Denmark, dies.	AD 1035
Death of Harthacnut, last Danish king of England.	AD 1042
King Macbeth of Scotland is killed by Malcolm Canmore, who later becomes king.	AD 1057
Harold, son of Godwine, and his brother Tostig fight the Welsh.	AD 1063
Harold is shipwrecked in Normandy.	AD 1064
Edward the Confessor sees the completion of Westminster Abbey.	AD 1065
Harold is king. Normans win battle of Hastings. William becomes king.	AD 1066

△ The Normans built castles to defend their newly won lands and subdue the conquered English. Each castle stood on an earth mound, or motte. A wooden tower was built on top. At the foot of the mound was a stockade, or bailey, inside which were stables, houses for soldiers, stores, and a kitchen.

△ *William of Normandy ruled England from AD 1066 to 1087. He claimed that Edward the Confessor promised him the throne in AD 1051. He also said that Harold (who was shipwrecked in France in AD 1064) had sworn to accept this.*

back his claim. This may or may not be true. Hardrada and William were both tough soldiers, and both prepared to attack England to seize the throne.

Two battles and a conquest

The Norwegians landed first, in the north of England. Harold defeated them at the battle of Stamford Bridge near York on September 25 AD 1066. Both Harold Hardrada and Tostig were killed. Then news came that William's ships had landed in Sussex, and Harold at once rushed south to fight them.

The crucial battle was fought only 19 days later, on October 14 at Senlac Hill, north of Hastings. The English, who fought on foot, resisted bravely as the Norman cavalry charged their wall of shields, and archers fired showers of arrows at them. In the end, Harold was killed, the shield wall broke, and the Normans won.

The Normans rule

William declared himself king. He was crowned in Westminster Abbey on Christmas Day. The English nobles lost their lands. French became the language of government. William and his barons built castles to guard their new land. A new age was beginning.

▷ *The story of William's invasion and the battle of Hastings is told in 72 scenes in the Bayeux Tapestry. The embroidery is about 20 in. wide and 76 yards long. It was made on the orders of William's half-brother.*

The people who lived during the late Middle Ages did not, of course, think they were "medieval" at all but modern. The term "medieval," which comes from the Latin word meaning "of the middle age," was only invented much later on, by historians and other scholars.

The Late Middle Ages

Richard I

The late Middle Ages stand in the gap between the Norman Conquest of England, in 1066, and the modern period, which begins with the Renaissance.

In many ways this time seems puzzling and remote to us today, full of armored knights, saints, pilgrims, gloomy castles, and muddy villages. The only heat came from open fires, and the only light from oil or candles. Time meant little, for there were very few clocks in use.

Life and faith

The vast majority of people all over the world lived and worked on the land. They depended entirely on what they could grow or catch, and if crops failed or hunting was bad, they would simply starve. Hunger was always a threat, and so were disease and war. In this world of fear and death, religion had a very important place.

By about AD 1000, Christianity had taken hold across nearly all of Europe, while the religion of Islam had spread across the Near East. These two faiths governed every part of people's lives and gave out harsh treatment to anyone who dared to question them.

Familiar sights

Yet the late Middle Ages also included many things that are familiar to us today. The first great cities, such as Venice and Constantinople, were growing, and many modern nations were forming. The idea of rule by parliament was developing, and the earliest universities were founded. People were beginning to introduce systems of banking. We can still see many fine medieval buildings today, from the cathedrals and castles of Europe to the temples and palaces of faraway Asia.

How did a medieval king control his realm? In Europe, few monarchs were rich enough to keep a standing army ready to put down a rebellion. Besides, most of their subjects lived in remote areas where bad roads made traveling slow and difficult, especially for large bands of soldiers.

Lords and Peasants

The answer was to share the land among royal supporters. The king gave grants of property, called fiefs, to his most powerful noblemen – the bishops, barons, and other strong knights. In return, the nobles promised to obey the king and to raise troops to fight for him whenever they were needed. Historians refer to this system of fiefs (or "feus" in Scotland) as "feudalism."

Feudalism touched every part of society, from top to bottom. The nobles granted portions of their estates to lesser lords or knights, who in turn rented plots of land to small farmers and peasants. The peasants paid the rent by laboring on their landlord's fields and giving him a share of what they grew themselves.

Peasants

The life of a peasant was hard – and often short. (The average lifespan of a European peasant in 1300 was only 25 years.) Peasants had to work every day except for Sundays and "holy days" (holidays), tending their animals and crops. Markets were usually far away, so if they didn't grow enough food they would probably starve. There was also the danger of death from disease or violence.

△ This stronghold of a Norman lord is well protected against attack. Around the lower area, called the bailey, runs a palisade (fence) of pointed stakes. The wooden tower (an early form of castle) above is built on a flat-topped mound called a motte.

△ *The medieval peasant owned almost nothing. The landlord owned the land and buildings in the manor, as well as all the animals and crops. He even owned the peasants' clothes.*

In the fields

These peasants are working in the fields surrounding their lord's castle. They are breaking up the soil with a plow pulled by an ox. At this time, the large majority of Europeans were peasants.

The manor

There were very few big towns in early medieval Europe, and at least 90 percent of people lived and worked in the countryside, on manors or estates belonging to their landlord. The farmland in the manor was divided into three sections, and the families were given plots in each one.

The lord of the manor had complete control of his little community. He took rent from the peasants living in his manor, in the form of produce and labor. He was the judge in the manor court, with the power to fine or imprison wrongdoers.

The castle

At the center of the manor was the lord's home. This might be simply a large house, built strongly of stone. A richer and more powerful lord might live in a castle, with room for knights and other soldiers. Kings and barons sometimes built a series of castles to impose their control over a wide area. More than 25,000 castles were built in Western Europe alone during the Middle Ages.

If an enemy army approached, the villagers could take shelter inside the castle, bringing their livestock and food stores with them.

△ *A highly ornate gold drinking goblet. Only a very wealthy person could afford costly items like this. Poorer people drank out of leather tankards or earthenware cups.*

> A good man was ther of religioun,/ And was a poore Person of a town,/ But riche he was of holy thought and werk.
> ### *THE CANTERBURY TALES,* GEOFFREY CHAUCER
> *Chaucer was a poet who lived at this time. The Canterbury Tales is his most famous work.*

Palestine lay at the eastern end of the Mediterranean Sea. This was the Holy Land, the most important place in the Christian religion, where Jesus Christ had been born and lived. When it was captured by Muslim armies in the 11th century the Christian powers in Europe set off to recapture it.

The Crusades

Arab Muslims had conquered Palestine in about AD 660, but they had still allowed Christian pilgrims to visit. However, when the Seljuk Turks swept down from central Asia and invaded Iran, Iraq, and then Palestine, they persecuted Christians. By 1078, they had seized the Holy City of Jerusalem and were even threatening Constantinople itself.

The First Crusade

The Byzantine emperor, a Christian monarch who lived in Constantinople, needed help. He turned to the pope, who in 1095 called for all Christians to start a holy war against the Seljuks.

Thousands rushed to join the Crusader armies. They crossed into Palestine and recaptured the important cities of Nicaea and Antioch. Jerusalem fell in 1099 after a desperate siege lasting six weeks, and the Crusaders took terrible revenge by slaughtering thousands of Muslims.

AD	
Seljuk Turks seize holy city of Jerusalem.	1078
First Crusade ends in retaking of Jerusalem (1099).	1096
Second Crusade ends in Christian defeat and loss of Jerusalem again.	1147
Saladin becomes leader of the united Seljuks.	1187
Third Crusade. Christians fail to regain Jerusalem.	1189
Crusader troops sack Constantinople.	1204
Children's Crusade ends in tragedy.	1212
European interest in recapturing the Holy Land begins to fade.	1291

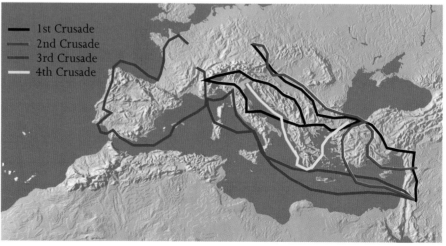

△ The routes taken by the First, Second, Third, and Fourth Crusades to the Holy Land, spanning a period of more than 100 years.

- 1st Crusade
- 2nd Crusade
- 3rd Crusade
- 4th Crusade

△ *At the end of the First Crusade, many knights stayed to guard the conquered land. They built fine castles and settled down to lead comfortable lives as colonists.*

▷ *Standards flutter in the breeze as Crusader knights board galleys and sailing ships in a Mediterranean port. Servants carry on baggage and supplies for the voyage to the Holy Land.*

The Second, Third, and Fourth Crusades

The easy existence of the newly victorious Christian forces made them weak. The Turks meanwhile grew strong again and struck back in 1144 by taking Edessa. Alarmed, the German and French kings answered the threat by leading fresh armies on the Second Crusade in 1147, but the Muslim forces quickly defeated them.

By 1187, the Muslims were united under a new leader – the wise and gallant Saladin. He launched his own holy war, or "jihad," against the European invaders, driving them out of Jerusalem. Once again, a Crusader army sailed for the Holy Land but failed to retake Jerusalem. In 1202, the Pope called for yet another expedition to seize Jerusalem. This was a greater disaster, because the Crusaders never reached Palestine. Greedy for money and loot, they decided to attack Constantinople instead. The capital of the Byzantine Empire was taken by storm and sacked in 1204, and the Christian emperor, whose plight had inspired the first Crusade, was killed.

The Children's Crusade began in 1212. Fifty thousand children set off from France and Germany for the Holy Land. Many died on the journey; many more were captured and sold as slaves in Africa. The Pied Piper legend may be based on the story of these children.

Richard I

Richard I of England and Philip II of France led the armies of the Third Crusade, setting sail for the Holy Land in 1189. Despite early success, the two leaders began quarreling and never recaptured Jerusalem. Richard was forced to make a treaty with the Muslim leader, Saladin, and return home.

Richard I

△ *The seal of the Christian knights who settled on the island of Sicily. They pledged to shelter and protect pilgrims traveling to Palestine.*

In 1167, a child called Temujin was born on the desolate plains of Mongolia. When the boy was nine, his father was murdered and his family was left poor and friendless.

The Mongol Empire

From this grim beginning, Temujin grew up to become one of the world's greatest conquerors. He was hailed by the Mongols as Genghis Khan – the "Universal Ruler."

The great khan

The Mongols were tough and violent and splendid horse riders. For centuries, the many Mongol clans, or groups, had fought among themselves. As Genghis Khan rose to power, he united these clans and organized them into a fearsome army.

In 1206, Genghis Khan became leader of all the Mongol people and began to build his astonishing empire. First, he defeated the neighboring Tanguts to the south. Then, in 1213, his massive army swept over the Great Wall into China. After destroying the troops of the

Birth of Temujin.	1167
Temujin becomes leader of all Mongols, with the title of Genghis Khan.	1206
Mongol armies begin invasion of China.	1213
Mongol armies invade and devastate Khwarizm.	1218
Death of Temujin.	1227
Ogodei, son of Temujin, becomes new khan.	1229
Mongol armies suffer first defeat at Ain Jalut.	1260
Kublai, grandson of Temujin, conquers southern China.	1276
Failure of Mongols' attempt to invade Japan.	1281

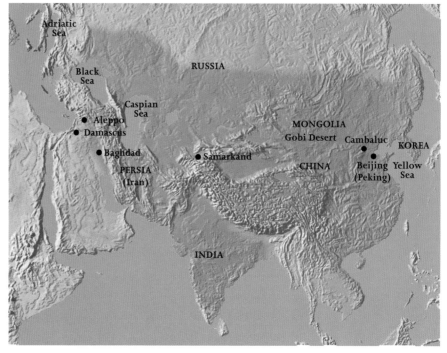

△ The mighty empire of the Mongols stretched from the Danube river in Europe in the west, across eastern Europe and Asia, to China in the east.

Mongol life

The Mongols lived on the flat, grassy steppes of Asia, wandering with their herds of sheep, goats, and cattle. They carried their tentlike felt homes, called yurts, around with them.

△ *Genghis Khan was a ruthless warrior, destroying entire cities and their populations during his conquests. Yet he succeeded in keeping the peace across his vast empire.*

Chin emperor, they marched on to Beijing. The emperor fled south, leaving the whole of northern China to the Mongols. When the Sultan of Khwarizm (modern Iraq and Afghanistan) killed a party of Mongol merchants in 1218, Genghis Khan's troops raged through Khwarizm, burning cities, plundering, and killing.

Into Europe

Genghis Khan died of a fever in 1227, but the Mongols continued to build the empire. The new khan was Ogodei (Temujin's son), who strengthened his hold on Khwarizm and China. Within 50 years, all of China's vast lands were under Mongol rule.

In 1236, Ogodei's son Batu set out on the most ambitious adventure yet. With an army of 150,000 men, he crossed the River Volga and invaded Russia. From here, Batu rampaged into Poland and Hungary and reached the shores of the Adriatic Sea. The Mongol Empire now stretched right across Asia and into Europe.

Batu was poised to sweep on into Western Europe, but events at home forced him to turn back. Ten years later the Mongols came west again. They sacked the cities of Baghdad, Aleppo, and Damascus, but again their leader was summoned back home.

△ *A Mongol warrior. With their tight discipline, nimble horses, and rapid shooting of arrows, the Mongols were terrifying enemies.*

▷ *A group of Arab merchants take shelter from the fierce midday heat. Their camel train is carrying goods from ports on the Red Sea to the Mediterranean coast.*

29

AD — 1100, 1200, 1300, 1400, 1500, 1600, 1700, 1800

"For God's sake, let us sit upon the ground and tell sad stories of the death of kings," says Richard II of England in Shakespeare's play. Being a medieval ruler was a dangerous business, especially in Britain.

Medieval Monarchs

Richard II himself was deposed in 1399 and savagely murdered, as was Edward II 50 years earlier. Henry II (1189) and Richard I (1199) were killed in battle, and John (1216) and Edward I (1307) died of disease.

The power of the barons

European kings saw themselves as chosen to rule by God, and they were crowned in magnificent religious ceremonies. They believed that they had complete power over their subjects and that anyone who rebelled against them was defying God's wishes. All the same, a king who was weak, unjust, or stupid could soon get into trouble with his powerful barons.

Many barons grew so strong that the monarch could not control them, and some even built up their own fiefs into small independent realms within a kingdom. They raised private armies, which they sometimes used to attack their neighbors and plunder their possessions and land.

The king's court

A wise king summoned his barons to court, where he could keep an eye on them. The royal court was the center of the kingdom, where the monarch showed off his wealth and power. Many courts were scenes of great magnificence. Frederick II, the Holy

c. 1170 — Henry II of England holds special court sessions to settle disputes.

c. 1180 — Andreas Capellanus writes a book called The Art of Courtly Love.

1215 — English barons force King John to sign the Magna Carta.

c. 1225 — The Roman de la Rose, the most famous troubadour poem, is written.

1241–1270 — Reign of "ideal" monarch, Louis IX of France.

1264 — English "commons" are summoned to the King's Council for the first time.

1295 — King Edward I of England calls first recognizable parliament.

c. 1400 — English Commons gain the right to introduce bills to Parliament.

△ *The magnificent coronation of Charles V. He became king of Spain in 1516 (he was the grandson of King Ferdinand and Queen Isabella of Spain), and three years later he was crowned Holy Roman Emperor. During his reign Charles ruled more countries than any other monarch in Europe.*

△ *Jousting in medieval times. Clad in a full suit of armor, knights on horseback competed in jousting matches, trying to knock each other to the ground with lances.*

Magna Carta

In 1215 the English barons forced the unpopular King John to sign a document now called Magna Carta (Great Charter). It protected the rights of nobles, and made sure no one was imprisoned without trial.

Roman Emperor (1220–1250) had a castle with golden floors, dancing girls, and exotic animals. Charles V of France (1364–1380) entertained 800 guests at his palace in Paris with a feast of 40 dishes.

However, the court was also the seat of government. The king's ministers and officers collected taxes and made laws. The monarch himself might also preside over special sessions to settle disputes between nobles and decide on grants of land.

Love and war

There were many pastimes for the royalty and nobles at court. The courtiers watched mock battles, or "tourneys," in which groups of knights fought each other. Not all games were so violent. On wet days, lords and ladies might sit indoors playing chess or backgammon, while card games (which were invented in China or India) became popular in Europe in the 1200s. A more daring pursuit was "courtly love," a sort of artificial love game with very strict rules. A knight declared his passion for a lady (probably married to someone else) and wrote her worshiping poems but rarely pursued his interest any farther.

"No free man shall be taken or imprisoned or dispossessed, or outlawed or exiled ... except by the lawful judgement of his peers or by the law of the land. MAGNA CARTA (1215)"

△ *King John, who was forced to sign the Magna Carta. Copies of the document, which tried to put an end to the king's abuse of his power, were distributed across England.*

During the Middle Ages, England became the dominant power in the British Isles. Yet for most of the period, her rulers were not English but French. The Normans came in 1066 and quickly formed England's ruling class.

AD

1800 · 1000 · 1100 · 1700 · 1200 · 1600 · 1300 · 1500 · 1400

Kingdoms of Britain

After the Normans came the Plantagenets, whose first king, Henry II, was crowned in 1154. The biggest part of Henry's realm was in France. His son, King Richard I, spent less than six months of his reign in England.

Henry II brought peace to England after years of civil war and unrest. He curbed the power of the barons and reformed the legal system. He also led several expeditions to France to try and expand his territories there. There were also closer neighbors to deal with. The English kings needed to stop invasions into English territory. In addition, control of the other nations of the British Isles allowed the English to earn more money by raising taxes.

Ireland
Henry II invaded Ireland in 1169, entered the capital Dublin, and forced the Irish rulers to accept him as overlord. After this, English settlers gradually took over the eastern part of the island, seizing land from Irish chieftains. English rule brought increased trade and prosperity to

Malcolm III becomes first king of a united Scotland.	1057
William I becomes first Norman king of England.	1066
Henry II becomes first Plantagenet king of England.	1154
English soldiers invade Ireland.	1169
Llewelyn II rules over most of Wales.	1256
Edward I completes conquest of Wales and begins castlebuilding.	1282
Edward I invades southern Scotland.	1296
Robert the Bruce defeats English at Bannockburn.	1314
English recognize Scottish independence.	1328

△ Robert the Bruce, leader of the Scots, inspired the Scots to a great victory against the English at Bannockburn in 1314. Over 10,000 English soldiers were killed.

△ Robert the Bruce. After the victory at Bannockburn, he drove the English out of Scotland by 1328, forcing them recognize Scotland as an independent country.

Welsh castles

Edward I built a chain of castles, including the one at Beaumaris (right), in the north of Wales, so that English troops could maintain his rule.

Ireland. This situation lasted until 1315, when a Scottish army landed in Ulster. After a long war, Ireland lay in ruins. England's power was weakened and never properly recovered, and the Irish chieftains won back most of their lands.

Wales

Norman barons had settled in the south of Wales, but in about 1215, the Welsh drove them out. They were united by Llewelyn the Great, their first national leader. By the 1250s, his grandson, Llewelyn, ruled most of the north and center of Wales. Edward I was determined to take control of the Welsh. Within ten years of coming to the throne, his armies had defeated Llewelyn and conquered most of Wales.

Scotland

The Scots caused the biggest problems for the English. In the 1200s, Scottish armies had made several border raids into northern England. Edward I was eager to conquer this dangerous and prosperous country. In 1296, he invaded and crushed the Scots at Dunbar. By 1305 he had defeated and killed the freedom fighter William Wallace. Defeat at Bannockburn by R obert the Bruce finally ended English success.

△ An Anglo-Irish cavalryman. By 1300 most of Ireland was under the control of the English.

Now's the day, and now's the hour; See the front o'battle lour! See approach proud Edward's power – Chains and slaverie.

SCOTS, WHA HAE, ROBERT BURNS

Robert Burns was a poet that lived in the 1700s. He wrote many patriotic Scottish poems.

△ The lion was seen as a symbol of English power. For over 200 years, English kings tried to impose their rule on the other nations of the British Isles.

The 14th century was filled with wars: in southeast Asia, the Siamese invaded Cambodia; Timur Lang, the last great Mongol leader, sacked Baghdad; the Ottoman Turks swarmed into eastern Europe; the Austrians fought the Swiss; the Portuguese fought the Castilians; and, in Germany, the nobles fought each other.

The 100 Years' War

The longest and most exhausting of these wars was between England and France. It lasted, off and on, until the middle of the 1400s and is known as the Hundred Years' War.

Two rivals

The conflict was a very complicated one. The Plantagenet kings of England also ruled a large part of France, while the rest belonged to the king of France. Both monarchs wanted to be the sole ruler of a united country. The French began to move into the English lands, seizing Normandy in 1204 and later taking charge of Gascony in the southwest.

There were plenty of other reasons for war. The French supported the Scots in their struggle against England. The English, in turn, claimed the throne of France when Charles IV died in 1328 and left no heirs.

The first phase: 1337–1360

Edward III of England dispatched his army to Normandy in 1337. He won a great sea battle at Sluys in 1340, as well as two land battles – at Crecy in 1346 and at Poitiers in 1356. He

▷ Edward, the oldest son of Edward III, was known as the Black Prince because he wore a suit of black armor. At the age of 16, he led a wing of the English army at the Battle of Crecy.

Edward III invades Normandy.	1337
English victory at the battle of Crecy.	1346
Treaty of Bretigny brings brief halt to the war.	1360
War breaks out again, and English lose territory in France.	1369
Henry V defeats French at the battle of Agincourt.	1415
Treaty of Troyes makes Henry V heir to French throne.	1420
Beginning of series of French victories, inspired by Joan of Arc.	1429
French drive English from all of France except Calais.	1453

▷ English troops lay siege to the French town of Troyes. The city gates have been shut and barred against them. English officials are trying to persuade the leaders of Troyes to surrender.

△ English and Welsh longbowmen could shoot as many as ten arrows per minute. It took much longer to reload the French crossbows.

took the port of Calais and captured the new French king, John the Good. But the English army was smaller than the French one, far from home and ravaged by disease and lack of food. Edward made a treaty with the French in 1360, granting him control of Gascony in return for giving up his claim to France's throne.

Mercenaries and rebels: 1360–1413

The peace lasted only nine years. In 1369, the war flared up again when English armies tried to establish a hold on Gascony and Aquitaine. They sacked the city of Limoges, slaughtering its inhabitants. But Edward slowly lost most of the land he had gained.

The final phase: 1413–1453

In 1413, England had a new and warlike king – Henry V. He renewed the English claim to the French throne, launching a fresh invasion in 1415. He won the battle of Agincourt against a much bigger French army. When Henry V died in 1422, the tide turned again. The French, inspired by Joan of Arc, won a series of battles. By 1453, they had driven the English from Maine, Gascony, and Normandy and the war was won.

Joan of Arc

The French troops were inspired by a young peasant girl called Joan of Arc. She claimed to hear voices from God, telling her to free the French from English rule. Joan was finally captured, tried by the English, and found guilty of witchcraft and heresy. On May 30, 1431, she was burned at the stake.

△ A longbowman's quiver of arrows. Other weapons used in the Hundred Years' War were crossbows, halberds (combined spear and axe), and cannons.

During the early part of the Middle Ages, few kings had permanent armies. In time of war, they ordered their barons and other nobles to call up people from their estates. Military service was one of the ways to pay the rent. The result was often a rabble of unskilled and terrified peasants.

The Age of Armor

The only quality troops were the knights and men-at-arms who fought on horseback. By the 1300s, however, many tenants had begun to pay their rents in cash. Kings and lords could use this money to hire professional soldiers, who were properly trained.

A knight usually came from an upper-class family. He began his training as a squire at the age of 14, learning to ride horses, wrestle, and fight with the sword and the lance. At about 21, the squire was made a knight at a special ceremony, where he promised to fight for good and punish evildoers.

c. 1100 — More extensive use of mail armor. Knights cover their arms and legs.

1147 — First recorded use of a stone-throwing trebuchet at the siege of Lisbon, Portugal.

1232 — Rockets first used in warfare (in China).

c. 1300 — Mail armor now often covered with steel plates.

1304 — First recorded use of a cannon by Arab troops.

c. 1400 — Knights wear full suits of jointed armor to cover the entire body.

c. 1420 — First steel crossbows in use.

▷ *When striking a castle, attackers battered at the gates with a heavy ram. They also constructed machines like cranes, which could lift soldiers over the walls and into the castle.*

△ *A knight in full armor. It was made of metal plates joined with straps and rivets to allow easier movement.*

Coat of arms

Each knight decorated his standard or shield with the heraldic symbols of his own coat of arms. This made it easier to identify the knight in full armor. Each coat of arms had its own unique design, made up of different colors, patterns, and objects or figures.

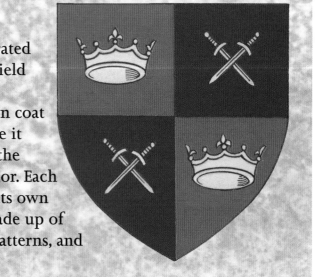

A knight rode into battle on a strong warhorse. He wore metal armor plates to protect his limbs and body, and a steel helmet, or basinet, on his head. On his left arm was a small curved wooden shield, and in his right hand was a long lance or a great double-edged sword.

The footsoldier

Footsoldiers had to be very tough. Unlike the mounted men, they would have to march as much as 19 miles a day, carrying all their equipment. Their simple leather boots soon grew soggy in wet weather, and lasted only a few weeks. Food was often scarce, as a large army soon ate everything in the surrounding countryside. Footsoldiers fought with narrow swords, short axes, or slashing blades set on long poles, called glaives.

△ *Some footsoldiers wore coats of mail, but most made do with a padded canvas tunic and a leather or metal helmet.*

Siege weapons

When the enemy took refuge inside a castle, there were two main ways of breaking down the defenses. One was to smash holes in the castle walls, often with the help of a battering ram hung from chains inside a shelter. The other was to dig a tunnel under the walls. The miners supported the roof of the tunnel with wooden beams. When it was complete, they built a big fire inside and ran away. As the props burned away the tunnel collapsed, bringing with it the foundations of the wall above.

◁ *This siege engine, known as a mangonel, was used to catapult stones at the walls of an enemy's castle.*

△ *An elaborate spearhead. In the mid-1300s, a new weapon came into use — a simple cannon that fired metal darts or stone balls.*

AD

1700 1800 1100 1200 1300 1400 1500 1600

"We see death coming into our midst like black smoke," wrote a Welsh poet in 1349. Bubonic plague was a deadly disease which brought death to most parts of Asia, North Africa and Europe. There was no known cure for this plague.

The Black Death

The plague started as a bloody swelling in the armpit or groin and quickly invaded the whole body. It was highly infectious and killed uncountable millions of people. Another writer of the time called it "the end of the world."

First outbreak of bubonic plague recorded in China.	1331
Plague reaches central Asia.	*c.* 1340
Genoese fleet brings plague to Europe.	1347
Plague reaches France and Britain.	1348
Spread of plague slows down.	1351
Second major outbreak throughout Europe and Asia.	1361
Beginning of third epidemic.	1375
Recurring outbreaks of plague in cycles of two or three years.	*c.* 1430

The Black Death begins

The infection probably began on the steppes, the grassy plains, of Asia. It was carried by fleas that lived on the fur of marmots and other rodents. Any hunter who had contact with one of these animals would almost certainly be bitten by the fleas and catch the plague. The steppe peoples were wanderers and soon spread the disease.

First reports of the epidemic came from China in 1331. Within 20 years, more than 30 million Chinese had died, and the plague had begun moving westward, reaching central Asia and India by 1340.

Into Europe

By now the fleas had found a new home, the fur of the black rat. The holds of most medieval cargo ships were full of rats, and so the plague began to spread even faster, by sea.

Traders sailed from the Black Sea across the Mediterranean, and then out into the Atlantic, taking the disease with them. In

△ Crowded medieval towns, with their cramped streets and open sewers, were ideal breeding grounds for disease. Corpses were left out in the road for people to collect, thus spreading the disease further. The doors of infected houses were locked and marked with a cross.

△ *Medieval paintings often depicted death as a skeleton, dancing and leading victims to their end.*

The Black Death spreads

Between 1347 and 1350, the Black Death raged across Europe and the Muslim world. As many as 1,000 people died daily in the port of Alexandria.

SCANDINAVIA
BRITISH ISLES
RUSSIA
FRANCE
SPAIN
ITALY
Constantinople
Alexandria

1347
1348
1349
1350

this way, it reached places as far apart as Sweden, Egypt, and Libya. In 1347, a Genoese fleet brought rats with the plague to the port of Messina in Sicily. Within a few weeks, thousands there had died. In terror, the citizens drove the ships out to sea again, but it was too late. The infection had taken hold.

Out of control

At the height of the epidemic, the daily death toll in Cairo, one of the world's largest cities, may have reached 7,000. In France and the British Isles, at least a third of the entire population perished. Everywhere there were scenes of chaos and horror. Wood for coffins was scarce, and victims had to be buried in mass graves, or "plague pits." When there was no space for graves, the rotting corpses were stacked in piles at the side of the road.

The plague returns

The epidemic began to slow down after about 1351. It had killed at least 25 million people in Europe and the Near East – one in three persons. In 1361, a second great outbreak swept across the land, followed by several more at intervals of two or three years. It was not until after another outbreak in the 1600s that the threat of the Black Death faded at last.

△ *Fleas living in the fur of the black rat carried the deadly plague virus across Europe. The rats lived close to humans, in the thatched roofs of people's homes.*

"Many died daily or nightly in the public streets: many others died at home.

GIOVANNI BOCCACCIO, ITALIAN POET, 1351

Boccaccio was an Italian poet and diplomat who lived between 1313 and 1375.

The Mongols completed their conquest of China in about 1270. For the first time the large country was united under the rule of a foreign power. The emperor was Kublai Khan, one of the grandsons of Genghis Khan, who governed very strictly.

Ming China

Kublai Khan forbade the Chinese from marrying into the Mongol race or speaking their language. They could not carry weapons, join the army, or hold positions of power. However, Kublai did give many important posts to foreigners. Among these was an Italian, Marco Polo, who arrived in Beijing in 1275.

Kublai Khan extends Mongol conquest of China.	1270
Marco Polo arrives in Beijing.	1275
Death of Kublai Khan.	1294
Chu Yuan-chang becomes first emperor of Ming dynasty.	1368
Death of Chu. His son Yung-lo becomes emperor.	1398
Seven exploratory voyages led by Zheng-ho.	1405–1433
End of the Ming dynasty.	1644

Marco Polo

Marco Polo was one of the first Europeans to visit the Mongol court. He impressed the khan, who appointed him governor of the city of Yangchow.

In his famous account of his adventures, Marco Polo described the wealth and prosperity which Kublai brought to China. There were huge granaries stocked with grain and a grand canal for bringing goods to the capital. The Yangtze River became a great highway for shipping, where boats were loaded with silk, gems, and other treasures ready for the Persian Gulf. However, some modern scholars believe that Marco Polo never actually went to China but wrote his account based on reading other peoples' descriptions.

▷ Kublai Khan receives Marco Polo at his court in Shangdu. Marco spent over 20 years in the khan's service, traveling all over China before returning home to Venice in 1295.

△ Running from the Pacific coast to central *Asia, the Great Wall* stretched for nearly 4,000 miles across China's northern border. Millions of men were forced to build it and thousands died.

Forbidden City

Beijing's Forbidden City was an area of elaborate palaces where only the servants of the emperor could enter.

The Ming emperors

After Kublai's death in 1294, Chinese people began to rebel against the harsh Mongol rule. By 1368, they had driven the foreigners out and the Ming dynasty had taken control. The first Ming emperor was Chu Yuan-chang, who had been a bandit, a soldier, and a monk. He restored Chinese pride and kept the country unified.

Chu and his successors turned Beijing into one of the greatest cities in the world, with the "Forbidden City" at its center. In the countryside, more land was plowed to grow more grain for food and cotton for clothing.

Walls and canals

The Chinese also had to protect themselves from further invasions from the north. They strengthened and extended the Great Wall as a barrier against attacks, fortified by garrisons of soldiers. To feed the troops, the Ming emperors also extended the Grand Canal, which carried 20,000 barges full of grain and other supplies over 1,000 miles.

The Chinese navy

Chu's son Yung-lo spent huge sums of money on exploration by sea. Fleets of 60 or more vessels made seven voyages into the Indian Ocean between 1405 and 1433.

By the 1430s, however, the Ming had grown suspicious of foreigners and travel. They ended the great voyages and banned overseas trade. Anyone who was caught dealing with foreign merchants was sentenced to death. China had closed itself off from the outside world once again.

△ Under the Ming emperors, art and literature flourished in China, most notably the making of the blue and white pottery still famous today as Ming porcelain.

There had been great cities in ancient times, such as Athens, Rome, Babylon, and Beijing. Most of these had fallen into ruin during the Dark Ages. Trade stopped between many towns, and thousands of people moved to the countryside to work on the land.

Towns and Trade

The later Middle Ages saw a return to the idea of living in cities. Peasants needed a market to sell their surplus produce. Craftworkers needed places to make and sell their goods. Merchants needed ports to receive cargoes. Bankers needed somewhere they could collect or lend out money.

Goods galore

Towns grew because trade grew. Goods traveled between East and West by ship or by the slower camel or horse transport overland. From China and the Indian Ocean came precious cargoes including silk, porcelain, and spices. From western Europe came iron, coal, cloth, and timber.

Ports such as Venice and Genoa became major trading centers. Their ships took goods all over the Mediterranean as far as London and Flanders. They also took part in the thriving trade in slaves, carrying men and women from Asia and Russia to be sold in North Africa and Europe.

London Bridge is the first stone bridge across the River Thames.	1209
Trading port of Gdansk founded.	1238
The first pure gold florin is minted in Florence.	1252
Milan becomes a city-state, governed by local nobles.	1277
Paris, with population of 150,000, is Europe's biggest city.	c. 1280
Venice defeats Genoa to gain control of eastern Mediterranean trade.	1380
Building of London's Guildhall, for all guild members.	1425
Founding of first important bank in France by Jacques Coeur.	1442

▷ *Inside a medieval shop, a butcher weighs customers' purchases on his scales. Anyone who cheated might find themselves in the stocks or fined.*

△ Banking probably developed in northern Italy, where moneylenders did their business from benches, or "banks." They charged customers interest for these loans.

△ Each occupation, including these blacksmiths, had its own guild. The guilds fixed prices and standards of work, and they made sure their members were well paid.

Gold florins

The bankers of the Italian city of Florence issued their own gold coins, called florins. This one is stamped with a lily, the city's emblem. It is the size of a fingernail. Cash was often too heavy and unsafe to carry around.

Freedom from feudalism

Towns, like villages, began as part of a lord's estate. Townspeople had to work for the lord and pay him rent. But as towns grew bigger and wealthier, the people wanted to be free from the old feudal ties. In England, the monarch gave citizens the right to govern themselves in return for a yearly payment. Such towns became boroughs, or burghs, able to make their own local laws and raise their own taxes.

Elsewhere, this struggle for freedom was more violent. In northern France and Belgium, there were armed rebellions against royal power. The free cities, or communes, often had to fight each other to keep their independence.

The guilds

The boom in prosperity and freedom was good for a town's craftworkers, and their numbers grew. Some cities had separate streets for each kind of trade – one for shoemakers, one for butchers, and so on. Each trade formed its own association, or guild. All workers in a guild trade had to go through a long and difficult training program. The guilds soon grew rich and powerful as they were able to set the prices that all the tradesmen in the guild were allowed to charge.

◁ The port of Constantinople, with its unique position between the continents of Europe and Asia, was an important trading center. Many of the rich trade routes between the Persian Gulf and the Black Sea passed through the city.

43

AD

1100 · 1200 · 1300 · 1400 · 1500 · 1600 · 1700 · 1800

In about 1300, a Turkish leader called Osman ruled a small kingdom in Anatolia (modern Turkey). His family name in Arabic was "Othman" and is better known to us today as Ottoman. Osman and his descendants were to build up one of the most important and long-lasting empires in world history.

The Ottoman Empire

The Ottoman Turks began to take over parts of the weak Byzantine Empire. The new empire was a strong Muslim answer to the power of Christian Europe in the west.

Osman founds small kingdom in Anatolia.	c. 1300
Ottoman clan gains control of all Anatolia.	1302
Beginning of Turkish advance. They capture Bursa, making it their capital.	1326
Ottoman Turkish armies cross into Europe, invited by Byzantine emperor.	1346
Turks defeat Crusader armies at battle of Nicopolis.	1396
Death of Timur Lang ends Mongol threat to Ottoman Empire.	1405
Mehmet II conquers Constantinople after a long siege.	1453

Beginnings of an empire
In 1346, a Byzantine leader hired some Ottoman troops to fight for him. This was a disastrous move. It allowed the Turks to cross the Dardanelles into Europe, where their fierce horsemen swiftly defeated the Bulgars and Serbs. In 1389, they crushed the Slav armies in Kosovo.

This greatly alarmed the Pope, who called for yet another crusade to turn back the Islamic threat to Europe. But the Ottomans massacred the crusading army at the battle of Nicopolis in 1396. They now ruled an area which stretched from Hungary to the Near East.

Timur Lang
When the Ottomans tried to expand eastward, there was a nasty shock in store for them. One of the rulers here was Timur Lang (Timur the Lame), who claimed to be a descendant of Genghis Khan. He had already conquered Persia and ravaged much of central Asia, including Russia and India, before the Ottomans attacked.

△ Sultan Mehmet II sent an army of over 150,000 soldiers, together with 300 ships and an array of huge cannons, to capture the city of Constantinople. Only 8,000 Byzantine troops were left to defend the capital. After eight weeks, the Turks broke through the massive city walls and completed their victory.

△ *An intricately carved doorway marks the entrance to an Ottoman mosque. After the fall of Constantinople, the city's Hagia Sophia church became a mosque.*

Timur Lang

Timur Lang was a ruthless leader. When he seized the city of Isfahan in 1387, he ordered his men to execute all 70,000 citizens and pile their heads in huge mounds outside the city walls.

Timur fell on the Turks like a hurricane, sacking their chief city in Anatolia, wiping out their army and capturing their leader. Then he began to loot their empire and break it up. That might have been the end of the Ottoman story, but in 1405, Timur died and the last of the Mongol kingdoms fell apart.

Rebuilding

Gradually the Ottoman dynasty put its empire together again. Under Sultan Murad I, the Turks regained parts of Greece and reached the borders of Hungary and Poland. The Ottoman army was now a highly trained force, led by troops of "janissaries," who were Christian slaves, and "spahis," or skilled mercenary soldiers.

After Murad died in 1451, his son, Sultan Mehmet II, nicknamed "the Conqueror" and "the Drinker of Blood," became sultan. Mehmet wanted, above all, to conquer the ancient city of Constantinople.

The fall of Constantinople

The fall of Constantinople in 1453 marked the end of Byzantine power and the start of a great Turkish advance. The city became the new Ottoman capital. Within 30 years, Mehmet had conquered most of southeastern Europe, including Greece and

> The empire of the world I say must be one. To make this unity, there is no place more worthy than Constantinople.
>
> SULTAN MEHMET II

△ *This Turkish battle standard would have been carried by the Ottoman armies. At the top is a crescent moon, the symbol of Islam.*

45

AD

After about 1450, the great nations of Europe began to emerge. For most of their history, they had consisted of small warring states, or had been invaded by powerful neighbors. Now, things were changing fast.

New Nations

The connection between France and England was broken at last. Spain and Portugal grew stable enough to found their great seagoing empires. Germany (part of the Holy Roman Empire) had strong leaders from the Habsburg dynasty.

Wars of the Roses

With the end of the Hundred Years' War in 1453, England was plunged into a fresh series of civil wars. The rivals were the two branches of the Plantagenet dynasty, York and Lancaster. In 1455, the ill Henry VI of Lancaster let his brother Richard of York rule as protector. When Henry recovered, Richard clung onto power but was defeated and killed.

In 1461, the Yorkists deposed Henry and Edward IV became king. In 1470, Edward fled and Henry became king again. In 1471, Henry was murdered. Another Henry reunified England when he defeated Richard III of York in 1485 and became Henry VII, the first Tudor monarch.

Cosimo de' Medici establishes his family as rulers of Florence.	1424
Sforza family seizes power in Milan.	1450
Beginning of power struggle in England between houses of York and Lancaster.	1455
Death of Charles the Bold allows Louis XI to seize Burgundy.	1477
Ivan III of Russia begins expansion of his kingdom by seizing Novgorod.	1478
Ferdinand II becomes king of Aragon.	1479
Henry Tudor wins battle of Bosworth to take the English crown.	1485
Muslims surrender Granada to Ferdinand and Isabella.	1492

△ King Ferdinand and Queen Isabella of Spain. Their marriage in 1492 united the two strong Christian kingdoms of Aragon and Castile.

46

△ Edward IV was the son of Richard, Duke of York. He took the English throne in 1461, after defeating the house of Lancaster at Towton, but was later ousted. He regained the throne again in 1471.

△ A Moorish nobleman and merchant. In 1492, the army of Ferdinand and Isabella forced the Moors to surrender Granada, the last Muslim region within the boundaries of Spain.

Italian city-states

Unlike Spain, Italy remained a divided country, split up into several states ruled by different powers. In the north were the wealthy city-states, such as Florence, Milan, and Urbino. The crest (right) belongs to the Sforza family, who ruled over Milan.

French expansion

France had beaten England, but it too faced rebellion. During the confusion of the long war, the French kings had lost much of their power to the nobles, but they had also built up a tough and well-trained standing army. When Louis XI came to the throne in 1461, he set out to bring his noblemen under control.

His chief enemy, Charles the Bold, died in battle in 1477, and after this, Louis was able to seize Burgundy, then most of southern France. The king unified much of the modern French state under a very strong monarchy.

A united Spain

In 1479, Ferdinand II became king of Aragon. His wife Isabella was already queen of Castile, so most of Spain came together under one pair of rulers. They wanted to establish the country as a Catholic stronghold. Non-Christians were driven from Spain with threats of imprisonment, torture, or death.

Ferdinand and Isabella also completed the great "reconquest" of Spain from Muslim control, which had begun over 400 years earlier. Within 20 years of the surrender of Granada, they had seized Navarre from France, and the country was ready to begin building its empire overseas.

△ The emblem of the House of York was a white rose; a red rose represented the House of Lancaster. The war between these two houses was known as the "Wars of the Roses."

> We read that we ought to forgive our enemies; but we do not read that we ought to forgive our friends.

COSIMO DE' MEDICI (1389–1492)

Cosimo Medici was a member of the powerful Medici family in Florence.

INDEX